LYME DISEASE

LYME DISEASE

ELAINE LANDAU

FRANKLIN WATTS
NEW YORK • LONDON • TORONTO • SYDNEY
A FIRST BOOK • 1990

Cover photographs courtesy of:
Photo Researchers: Margaret Durrance,
Inset: Scott Camazine.

All photos courtesy of: Photo Researchers: pp. 17 (John Moss),
18, 21, 22, 41, 42, 48 (all Hank Morgan/Science Source), 25
(Alan Carey), 27 (Steve Maslowski), 28 (Nick Bergkessel), 30
(Scott Camazine), 32 (John Serrao), 33 (Pat and Tom Leeson), 34
(Molly Adams), 37 (Richard Hutchings), 39 (John Radcliffe Hospital),
45 (Suzanne Szasz), 46 (Marc Tulane), 51 (Dailloux/Rapho),
52 (Will and Deni McIntyre/Science Source), 54 (Dana Hyde).

Library of Congress Cataloging-in-Publication Data

Landau, Elaine.
Lyme disease / by Elaine Landau.
p.   cm. — (A First book)
Includes bibliographical references.
Summary: Discusses the study, origins, symptoms, treatment
and control of Lyme disease.
ISBN 0-531-10931-3
1. Lyme disease—Juvenile literature.   [1. Lyme disease.]
I. Title.   II. Series.
RC155.5.L36   1990
616.9′2—dc20   89-70514   CIP   AC

For Norman

ALSO BY ELAINE LANDAU

Alzheimer's Disease
Black Market Adoption and the Sale of Children
The Sioux
Surrogate Mothers
Tropical Rain Forests Around the World
We Have AIDS

CONTENTS

LYME DISEASE

THE PUZZLE

It happened on a sizzling hot August day. Twelve-year-old Christopher stood on a swimming pool diving board in his northern New Jersey town. He paused before diving. Suddenly, a strong bolt of headache pain struck the left side of Christopher's head. It seemed to come from out of nowhere. The young boy later recalled how at one moment, he'd felt fine, and then the next, his head throbbed with pain. Christopher broke out in a cold sweat. He felt nauseous and his body ached all over.

At first, Christopher's family and doctor thought he had a bad case of the flu. Yet something else was wrong. Time passed, but Christopher's symptoms remained. His doctor didn't understand why. He couldn't find any medical reason for Christopher's illness.

Christopher tried to continue leading a normal life. He attended school regularly. Christopher enjoyed sports and being outdoors, and he was determined not to give up any of his other activities. But several months later, the situation worsened. Christopher experienced an extremely sharp pain in his right knee. It happened while he was on a backpacking trip with his father and two brothers. The pain was so severe that Christopher could barely walk.

After returning home, Christopher's knee felt even worse. His parents took him to a number of doctors. Unfortunately, no one was able to pinpoint Christopher's baffling ailment. A bone specialist from a nearby city diagnosed Christopher's condition as an inflamed kneecap. The doctor prescribed aspirin for Christopher and had him begin physical therapy.

But nothing seemed to help. Christopher grew weaker, and eventually needed crutches to walk. He often felt tired and his muscles were sore. After a while, Christopher found it difficult to even carry his school books. By now, his right leg was partially *paralyzed.* At times, Christopher seemed to show some improvement. Then, unfortunately, there would be relapses and he'd become extremely ill again.

Christopher's family continued to seek the help of different doctors. Finally, after another series of tests,

Christopher was correctly diagnosed. Now he was given the proper medication. And after nearly eighteen months of suffering, Christopher's condition began to improve.

The strange illness that had struck Christopher and puzzled so many doctors was Lyme disease.

THE MYSTERY'S HISTORY

The first reports of Lyme disease occurred in November 1975. At that time, two Connecticut mothers called the Connecticut State Health Department—each told a similar story. Both women had children who had been recently diagnosed as having juvenile rheumatoid *arthritis*. Naturally, the women were upset. Rheumatoid arthritis is an extremely painful illness that can lead to lifelong suffering.

The health department officials were alarmed as well, but for a different reason. The children whose mothers had called weren't the only ones stricken with the disease. A number of other children as well as adults in the town of Lyme, Connecticut, had also been diagnosed as having it.

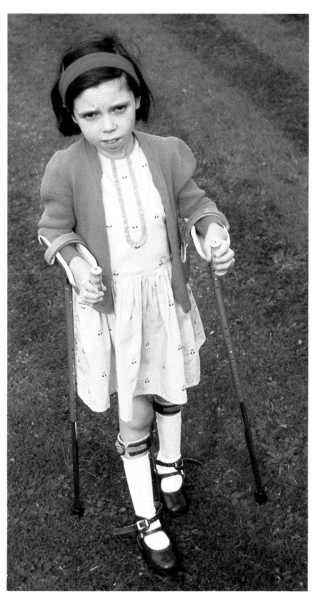

This young girl suffers from rheumatoid arthritis. Lyme disease has frequently been mistaken for this ailment.

Lyme disease research continues. Here
Dr. John Anderson, director of the Connecticut
Agricultural Experiment Station in New Haven,
records lab data. At the lab, ticks and blood
are analyzed for Lyme disease.

The health department officials suspected that something might be wrong in the region. They thought that perhaps people might have unknowingly been exposed to an environmental *toxin*. Another possibility was that an *epidemic* of a new disease—one that had been wrongly diagnosed as rheumatoid arthritis—was beginning there.

Health department officials contacted Dr. Allen C. Steere, a medical expert from Yale University. Dr. Steere had also done research on epidemics for the U.S. Centers for Disease Control in Atlanta, Georgia. Steere became interested in learning more about this strange outbreak of arthritis. He agreed to investigate the Connecticut mystery.

Along with his research team, Allen Steere discovered that the disease symptoms had occurred in three Connecticut towns. All the locations were within the eastern section of the state. The towns were Lyme, Old Lyme, and East Haddam—communities near one another on the east bank of the Connecticut River.

Generally, juvenile rheumatoid arthritis tends to be a rare disease. Under normal circumstances, only one out of 100,000 children will be affected by it. Yet the incidence of the disease in the three Connecticut towns seemed astoundingly high. The number of reported cases of this disease had been over 100 times more than the average rate at which juvenile rheumatoid arthritis usually occurs.

There were other curious aspects about the outbreak as well. The cases seemed to appear in unusual patterns. The vast majority of the victims lived in heavily wooded areas. Many of those stricken also lived quite near each other. It was clear to Dr. Steere that other factors were involved. At that point, he knew he wasn't just dealing with rheumatoid arthritis. Something else had to be happening.

Dr. Steere had few clues to lead him to an answer. But he was still able to draw some important conclusions from the available evidence. He learned that this new disease was not especially *contagious.* In some instances, several members of the same family might be stricken. However, they'd come down with symptoms in different years. He also found that in most cases he studied, the individuals first became ill during the summer, from June through September. In addition, Dr. Steere noted that most of the patients recalled having a skin rash that had appeared before the arthritislike symptoms began. This told him that there was probably an insect involved.

Health department staff members trap ticks to test for Lyme disease. This will help them determine how many ticks in a given area are infected.

*At the Agricultural Experiment Station in
New Haven, Connecticut, these ticks will be
examined for Lyme disease. As adult ticks,
they have eight legs with which to cling
to the host they feed on.*

The patients' descriptions of the red rash were strikingly familiar. Because the rash formed on various areas of the patients' bodies, the researchers thought that it was probably from the bite of a crawling, rather than flying, insect.

Dr. Steere's research led him to believe that the ill people in Connecticut were not suffering from rheumatoid arthritis. Instead, he realized that he was dealing with a different disease—one that was transmitted through an insect. Steere named the illness Lyme disease after the town in which its initial outbreak occurred.

LYME DISEASE

Lyme disease is an infection caused by a bacterial organism. The microscopic spiral-shaped organism responsible for Lyme disease is called a *spirochete*. Its scientific name is *Borrelia burgdorferi*.

The spirochete that causes Lyme disease is spread to humans through the bite of a tiny infected *tick*. This tick is so small that it's only about as big as a speck of pepper. In the eastern and midwestern United States, the tick that spreads Lyme disease is often found on the white-tailed deer. For this reason, it is commonly called a deer tick. The deer tick's scientific name is *Ixodes dammini*.

A deer tick is much smaller and more difficult to see than the better known dog tick that is often found on pets. In some regions in which Lyme disease is common, about 40 percent of the ticks in the area may be infected.

White-tailed deer, after which the deer tick is named, are among the most common deer in North America. The deer's tail is brown on top and white underneath.

In other areas, 80 or 90 percent of the ticks may be infected. The infected ticks that spread Lyme disease generally live in or near wooded areas. They are often found in tall grass or in bushes and shrubs.

The ticks that spread Lyme disease are *parasites*. This means that they feed off a living host. Among the ticks' most common hosts are deer, mice, birds, dogs, bears, opossums, chipmunks, gray squirrels, horses, racoons, and, of course, human beings.

When a host is bitten by an infected tick, spirochetes first enter its skin. There the organisms multiply and spread into the bloodstream. From the bloodstream, they infect the tissues of the host animals.

In recent years, Lyme disease has been spreading throughout the country. According to the Centers for Disease Control, Lyme disease has now become the most common tick-borne disease in America. Most of the Lyme disease cases have been concentrated in specific areas of the country. The most heavily hit regions have been the coastal Northeast, northern California and Oregon, and Wisconsin and Minnesota.

On the West Coast of the United States, Lyme disease is transmitted by a different tick. This tick is a close cousin of the eastern tick *Ixodes dammini*. The West Coast tick's scientific name is *Ixodes pacificus* (like the Pacific Ocean).

Both ticks have a two-year life cycle. An adult female tick lays its eggs in the early spring. About a month later,

Raccoons are among the smaller animals that serve as hosts for the deer tick. Here a female raccoon and her cubs rest in their den.

White-footed mice, sometimes called deer mice,
are common hosts of the deer tick. There are
over fifty different types of white-footed mice.
They can survive in many varied environments
such as mountains, forests, and deserts.

the eggs hatch into free-living larvae. The larvae are tiny, flat, six-legged organisms.

The larvae wait on stalks of tall grass and shrubs for animals to pass. Then they attach themselves to a host. It's usually a small animal like the white-footed mouse. Most ticks are not born with the spirochete that causes Lyme disease. Instead, they acquire the Lyme disease bacteria by feeding on an animal host that has already been infected by another tick.

During the summer, larvae only feed once on their host's blood. The feeding lasts for a period of two days. The larvae gorge themselves and swell up. Then, as the weather begins to turn colder in autumn, the larvae enter a resting stage.

The following spring, the larvae *molt*. This means that they shed their outer covering to enter the second stage of their life cycle. After molting, they turn into eight-legged creatures called nymphs. The nymph is still not a fully developed adult tick.

While in the nymphal stage, the tick attaches itself to an animal host, usually a small animal. This time the tick will feed for two to four days. At this point in their development, the ticks are also most likely to attach themselves to human beings. It may be interesting to note that the deer tick is one of the few ticks that bite humans before its fully developed adult phase.

These are three deer ticks. A male, a female,
and a smaller tick in its nymph stage.

At summer's end, the ticks molt again. This time the nymphs turn into adult ticks. Adult ticks are usually found in tall grass, and easily attach themselves to larger animal hosts. Adult ticks may feed on a variety of animal hosts including humans. But they are frequently found on the white-tailed deer.

Soon after the female tick firmly attaches herself to the animal host, the male and female tick mate. The male tick dies soon after mating. The female lives through the winter in order to lay her eggs. The eggs hatch in the spring. Then the cycle repeats itself.

People are at greatest risk of getting Lyme disease from June to August. That's because during this period, the nymph form of the tick is active. This is also the season when people tend to spend more time outdoors.

Ticks that carry Lyme disease also exist outside of the United States. There have been reported cases of Lyme disease in Europe, Australia, Asia, and Africa. In fact, Lyme disease has cropped up on every continent except Antarctica.

Most people tend to think of this illness as a new disease. However, undiagnosed cases of Lyme disease have actually been found throughout medical history. Outbreaks of the disease are known to have taken place as long ago as 1887 in Australia and 1909 in Sweden.

Scientists think the disease probably spread from Europe to the United States. It might have been brought to

These girls on a nature trail enjoy a warm-weather outing during the summer. Unfortunately, the deer ticks are active then as well. Opposite: During the year, birds may migrate or fly to different regions of the country. They do this to avoid unfavorable weather or a lack of food. Unfortunately, birds carrying infected deer ticks on their backs have spread Lyme disease to new areas.

People wishing to enjoy the beauty and privacy of forest areas have built homes in once heavily wooded regions. As a result, human beings have more readily become hosts for infected deer ticks.

America through infected ticks hitching rides on birds. In addition, *migratory* birds might be somewhat responsible for the disease's spread to various areas of the United States.

Another factor that may have helped to spread the disease is the vast increase in the number of deer, a common host of infected ticks. Lyme disease has sometimes been called the "suburban disease" because in recent years so much suburban housing has extended into areas that were once heavily wooded.

To date, more than 13,000 cases of Lyme disease have been reported. Because Lyme disease is tricky to diagnose, the disease may be even more widespread than is presently known. In some areas, the disease is underdiagnosed and underreported. In any case, Lyme disease is now the most common tick-transmitted disease in the world.

WHEN IT STRIKES

Anyone who lives in or visits an area where Lyme disease occurs can possibly become infected. Lyme disease affects both males and females. People of all ages are susceptible (able to become infected). A considerably large number of children have had Lyme disease. This may be largely because children spend much of their time playing outdoors in wooded or grassy areas.

Wildlife, such as deer, aren't affected by Lyme disease. However, domestic animals, such as dogs and cats, can get the disease. Infected dogs may run high fevers and develop arthritis. Cats usually do not become as ill.

The symptoms of Lyme disease vary considerably. People tend to experience this infection in different ways. There are some common symptoms though that affect

*Pets that spend time outdoors can be bitten
by deer ticks infected with Lyme disease.
However, the disease isn't fatal and can be
cured when properly treated by a veterinarian.*

most people with Lyme disease. Usually, the symptoms tend to appear in three stages.

Up to one month after the tick bite. Often the first symptom of Lyme disease is a rash. The rash tends to have a bright red outer border surrounding a clear spot at its center. Because it looks like a target bull's-eye, the rash is frequently called the bull's-eye rash. The rash usually first appears at the exact site at which the tick bit its victim. However, in some cases, the rash crops up on several parts of the body at once. And not everyone gets the rash. About 20 to 30 percent of Lyme disease victims never experience the rash at all.

During this early stage of the disease, many people with Lyme disease feel as though they have the flu. They may suffer from headaches, nausea, and tiredness. Experiencing both chills and fever is also common. There may be muscle and joint pain, too.

Several weeks to several months after the tick bite. At this point, the symptoms of untreated Lyme disease tend to worsen. Lyme disease victims may develop heart symptoms such as a slow heartbeat. This may be accompanied by dizziness and/or shortness of breath. By now, the infection may have already spread to the person's central nervous system. There may be numbness, tingling, and facial paralysis. Headaches, memory loss, irritability, and sleeplessness are also common during this period.

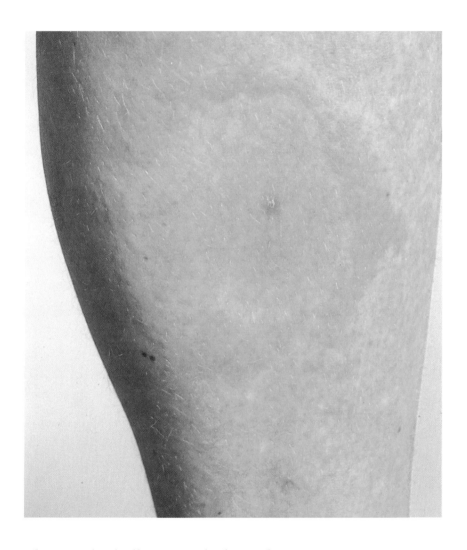

The circular bull's-eye rash shown here is a common early symptom of Lyme disease. In some cases, the rash may spread until it covers an area on the body the size of a Frisbee.

Months to years after the tick bite. This can be the most serious and severe stage of untreated Lyme disease. Stricken individuals may suffer from extremely painful arthritis in their joints and limbs. These flare-ups, which may last from a few days to a few weeks, can strike at any time. Usually, the joint most commonly affected by Lyme arthritis is the knee. Numbness in the arms or legs may also develop because the disease can affect the nerves in those areas. In rare instances, Lyme disease has also affected an individual's eyes and vision.

Pregnant women infected with Lyme disease may be especially at risk if left untreated. Lyme disease can cause serious birth defects in unborn children. In some cases, babies have been born temporarily blind and/or with webbed fingers. Congenital heart damage can occur. Lyme disease has also been responsible for premature births and *miscarriages*. At times, it has even caused the death of newborn infants.

Whenever possible, Lyme disease should be treated immediately. Humans as well as pets with Lyme disease are usually given *antibiotics*. An antibiotic is a medication used to destroy the disease-producing spirochetes within the body.

The longer the symptoms remain untreated, the more difficult it becomes to cure the disease. Some Lyme disease patients remain untreated because they've been incorrectly diagnosed. Because of its varied effects and its

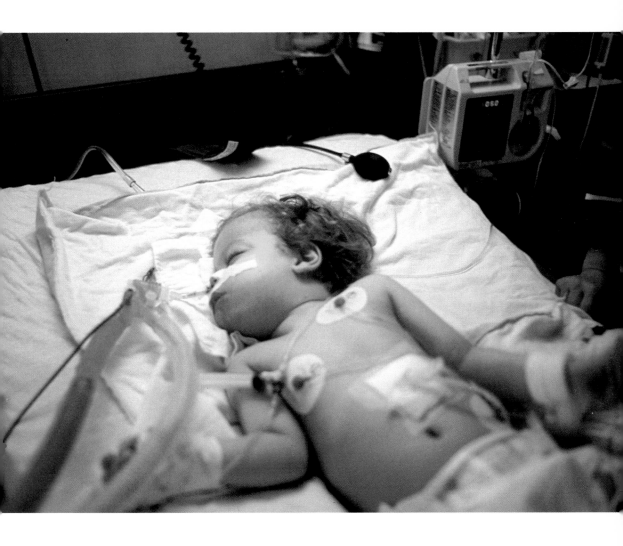

*Pregnant women infected with Lyme disease can
transmit the disease to their unborn baby.
This is Jamie Forschner, the first person believed
to have contracted the disease in this manner.*

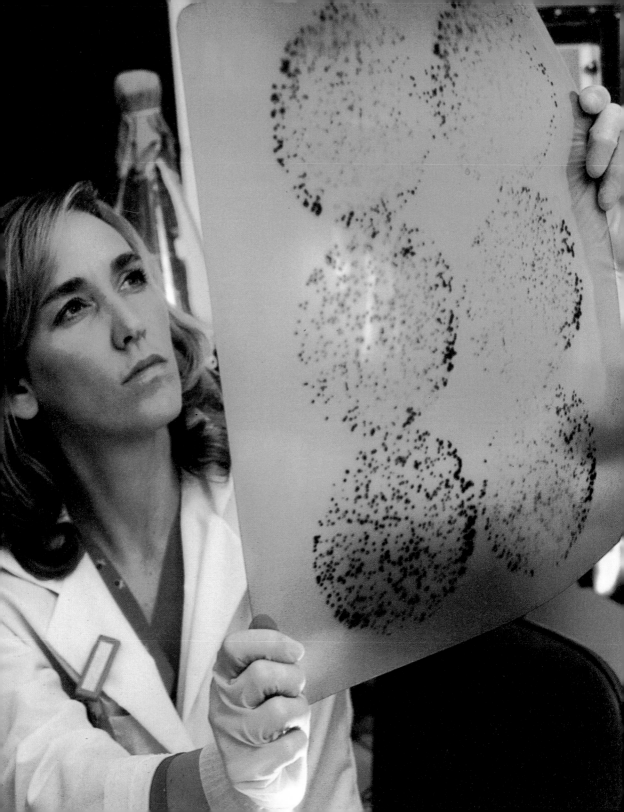

resemblance to other diseases, Lyme disease has often been called the "great imitator."

Although some untreated Lyme disease victims may improve on their own, not all do. If the disease remains untreated long enough, there may be permanent damage to the joints or nervous system. However, Lyme disease is easily cured if treated early on, and it can still be treated and improved in the late stage of the infection.

A medical researcher studies a bacterial virus. Research such as this may lead to the development of new methods for detecting and treating Lyme disease in the future.

PROTECTION

In numerous areas, Lyme disease has affected large numbers of people. For example, on some islands just off the coast of Massachusetts, nearly half of all residents were infected. On Fire Island, a beautiful woodland and beach area in New York, fifteen public park employees came down with the disease. This amounted to 20 percent of the staff.

It's important that people do their best to protect themselves from Lyme disease. The following guidelines may be especially useful in avoiding the disease.

1. If possible, try to avoid tick *habitats*. This would include wooded areas as well as tall grass and brush. It is important to remember that Lyme disease is *not* restricted to these areas. People have become Lyme disease victims walking across their front lawn or playing in their backyard.

These boys would be better protected against tick bites if they were wearing long-sleeved shirts.

2. Wear long pants. The pant cuffs should be tucked into socks. Wear closed shoes instead of sandals. People working in gardens should wear long sleeves.

3. Choose light-colored clothing. Ticks are dark; they'll be easier to spot on light fabrics.

4. Spray insect repellent on your clothing. A repellent that contains the substance DEET (diethyltoluamide) is considered most effective. Ticks are repelled by this ingredient. If you own a dog or cat, make certain the animal has a tick collar.

5. After you've been outdoors, brush off your clothes before reentering the house. Inspect what you're wearing for ticks. Check your pet for ticks if it's been outdoors with you.

6. If you've gone hiking or spent some time outdoors in an area where Lyme disease is common, don't wear your outdoor wear at home. This will reduce the risk of exposing other family members to Lyme disease.

7. When you undress, check your body for ticks. Pay special attention to the groin, back, armpits, and head. At times, deer ticks may crawl on a person for several hours before sinking in for a blood meal.

What's wrong with this picture?
Do you know what this hiker should
have worn for better protection
against Lyme disease?

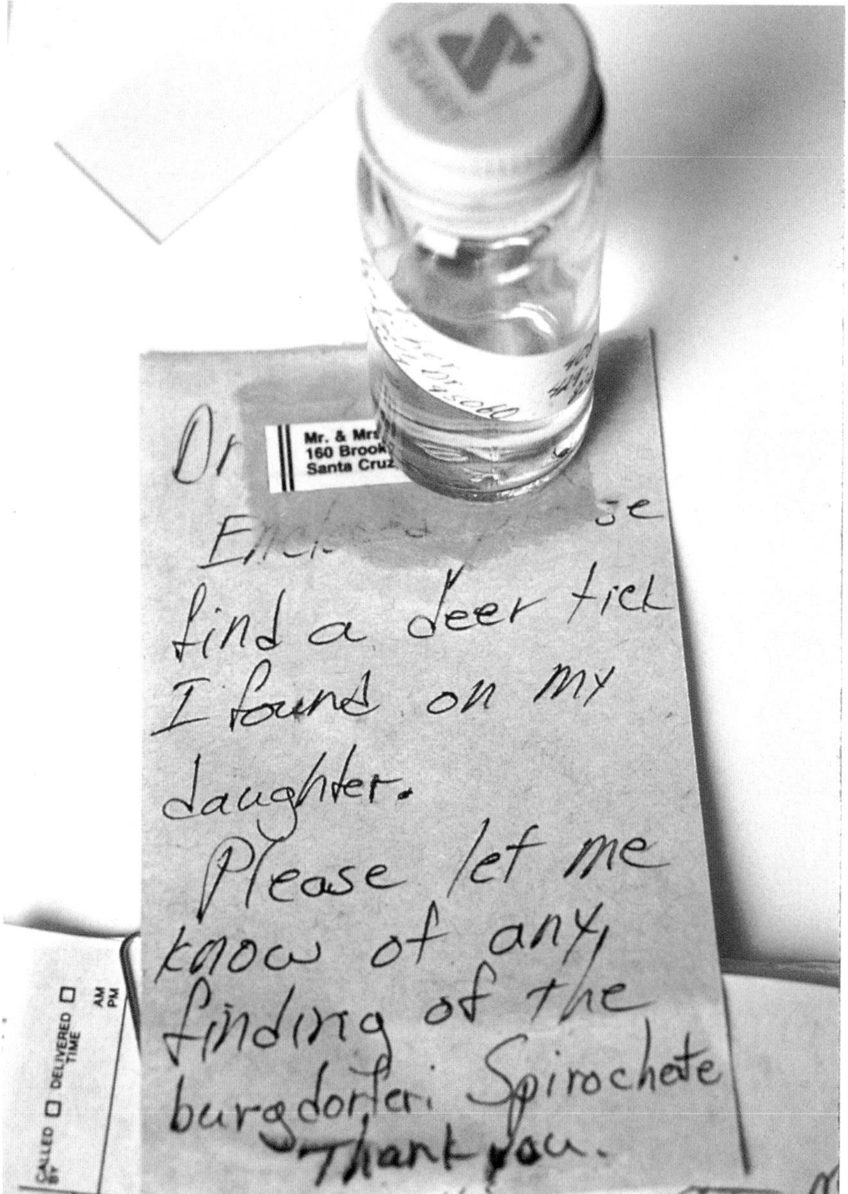

Mr. & Mrs
160 Brook
Santa Cruz
find a deer tick
I found on my
daughter.
Please let me
know of any
finding of the
burgdorferi Spirochete
Thank you.
CALLED BY
DELIVERED
TIME
AM
PM

8. If a tick is attached to your body, remove it with tweezers. Gently tug repeatedly at the site at which the tick entered the skin. Do not twist the tick. Grasp the tick as close to the skin as possible. As the tick is pulled out, make sure that its mouth parts do not remain in the skin. Wash the bite thoroughly. Record the date and where on your body you were bitten. Keep the tick in a jar for possible later identification by a laboratory.

9. If you think you have the Lyme disease rash, contact your doctor or clinic immediately. And take the tick you saved with you.

10. Within a month of a tick bite, remain alert for symptoms of the disease. This would include tiredness and generally not feeling well.

11. Be sure to mention to your doctor that you're concerned about Lyme disease.

12. If you're treated for Lyme disease, take the antibiotics for the full number of days prescribed. Do not discontinue use on your own once you begin to feel better.

A mother who found a tick on her young daughter sent it to the Agricultural Experiment Station in New Haven, Connecticut, to be examined for Lyme disease.

THE FUTURE

At present, the outlook for Lyme disease is still uncertain. Scientists are working on a vaccine to protect people and domestic animals from the disease. Researchers have already successfully immunized hamsters against Lyme disease. Tests for a vaccine for dogs are under way. Until a vaccine for people is perfected, early treatment is the best defense against the infection.

Researchers are also developing new tests to better diagnose Lyme disease. Work has been done to produce a urine analysis test for this purpose. In addition, the Food and Drug Administration has approved a blood test to detect Lyme disease that can be done in a doctor's office, and only takes about fifteen minutes.

Other research is under way to find a means to control the tick population. Ridding the countryside of white-

Research to perfect still better tests
for identifying Lyme disease continues.

tailed deer—a major host for adult ticks—would be nei-
ther humane nor effective. Besides, the ticks might easily
soon find an equally desirable host.

There hasn't been a great deal of success in using
chemical sprays to combat ticks either. The problem lies
in finding a way to place the tick in contact with the
chemicals. Often the vegetation acts as a barrier. Although widespread spraying would effectively destroy the
ticks, it would cause serious environmental damage also.

One somewhat successful chemical method involves
laying down cotton balls containing a pesticide. The pesticide used is not harmful to mammals, but it kills the
ticks. Field mice find the cotton and pad their nests with
it. Although they remain unharmed, the ticks exposed to
the toxin die. This method has been helpful in some small

Some experts claim that the early
tests for Lyme disease were not
very accurate. At times, there
has been a nearly 80 percent error
rate. People who had actually
been infected with the disease were
told that they didn't have it.
It is hoped that more research
will correct this problem.

A park ranger speaks with a group of schoolchildren.
Public health departments and parks have stressed
the importance of knowing about Lyme disease.

residential areas and parks. However, it is too costly to use on a large scale. Other research to control the spread of Lyme disease involves finding a weak link in the deer tick's two-year life cycle.

Meanwhile, health departments across America have mounted extensive public awareness campaigns to combat Lyme disease. It's important for people to learn as much as they can about the illness. Until Lyme disease is conquered, knowledge remains our best safeguard.

GLOSSARY

Antibiotic: A medication used to treat infectious diseases

Arthritis: A disease of the joints that causes pain, stiffness, and swelling. Rheumatoid arthritis is one of the two chief forms of arthritis

Bacteria: Simple, one-celled organisms. Some forms of bacteria are helpful, some are harmless, others cause disease

Bacterial disease: A disease caused by microscopic one-celled organisms that multiply rapidly in living tissue, damaging or killing it

Contagious: Transmission of a disease by direct or indirect contact

Epidemic: Outbreak of a disease that affects many people at one time

Habitat: The place where an animal or plant naturally lives

Migration: The travel of animals to different areas that offer better living conditions

Miscarriage: The unplanned-for end of a pregnancy before the baby is able to survive out of its mother's womb

Molt: To shed outer covering

Paralysis: A condition characterized by loss of the ability to move. Paralysis may be temporary or permanent

Parasite: An animal or plant that lives off of another animal or plant

Pesticide: A chemical used to restrict or destroy pests

Spirochete: A microscopic spiral-shaped organism that causes disease

Tick: A tiny, oval-shaped animal that lives off other animals; some ticks transmit diseases

Toxin: A substance that is poisonous when introduced into the body

FOR FURTHER READING

Ahlstrom, Mark. *The Whitetail.* Mankato, Minn.: Crestwood House, 1983.

Donahue, Parnell and Helen Capellaro. *Germs Make Me Sick: A Health Handbook for Kids.* New York: Knopf, 1975.

Horton, Casey. *Insects.* New York: Franklin Watts, 1984.

Saintsing, David. *The World of the Deer.* Milwaukee: Garth Stevens, Inc., 1987.

Selsam, Millicent E. *Where Do They Go? Insects in the Winter.* New York: Scholastic, 1984.

Silverstein, Alvin and Virginia Silverstein. *Mice: All About Them.* New York: Harper & Row, 1980.

Tiger, Steven. *Arthritis.* Englewood Cliffs, N.J.: Julian Messner, 1986.

INDEX

ABOUT THE AUTHOR

Elaine Landau received her BA degree from New York University in English and journalism and a master's degree in library and information science from Pratt Institute.

Ms. Landau has worked as a newspaper reporter, an editor, and a youth services librarian. She has written many books and articles on contemporary issues for young people. Ms. Landau lives in Sparta, New Jersey.